The Ultimate Pet Guide

Jean Coppendale

QEB Publishing

First published in the United States by
QEB Publishing, Inc.
23062 La Cadena Drive
Laguna Hills, CA 92653

www.qeb-publishing.com

Library of Congress Control Number: 2007931762

ISBN 978 1 59566 483 9

Written by Jean Coppendale
Edited by Gill Munton
Consultancy by Michaela Miller
Designed by Susi Martin
Photography by Jane Burton (except p7 top image by
Getty Images, and vegetables on page 80 by Chris Taylor)

Publisher Steve Evans
Creative Director Zeta Davies
Senior Editor Hannah Ray

Printed and bound in China

Contents

Puppies

Your first puppy

▶ **Spaniel puppies**

A puppy is a great pet. You can play together and have lots of fun. But puppies are not toys. They can get hurt easily, so you should treat them very gently.

When you play with your puppy, don't be rough—if you hurt it, your puppy might bite. If your puppy trusts you, you will have made a loyal friend for life.

▲ A Golden Lab puppy

◀ A Boxer puppy

▶ A Husky puppy

Puppies are very cute—but puppies grow up into dogs. Most dogs like to play, but a full-grown dog might not be as cute and playful as a puppy.

Which puppy?

There are all kinds of puppies. Some are big and some are small. Different types of dog each have their own needs and personalities.

▲ **Small breeds like this terrier can be very active and may bark a lot.**

Puppies are different shapes and sizes

◄ **Golden Lab puppies grow into big dogs.**

▶ **Bull Mastif puppies will need a lot of exercise.**

Big dogs might need extra exercise while a clever, small dog might get bored quickly and want to play all the time.

▲ **Dogs with long hair like this Pomeranian will need a lot of brushing.**

Parent Points

When choosing a puppy, go to a reputable breeder or animal shelter. Seeing the puppy with its mother will give you the best idea of its eventual size. Avoid pet stores and want ads. Ask your local veterinarian for advice. A puppy should be at least eight weeks old before it leaves the litter and its mother.

If you are adopting a dog from a shelter, the staff there can help you choose one with the right temperament and background to live with a child.

Look for an active puppy that has a shiny coat, clear eyes, a clean bottom, and a moist, cold nose.

Lots of dogs

These dogs are all **purebred** dogs.

▲ Collie

▲ **West Highland White terrier**

▲ Afghan hound

◀ **Chihuahua**

▼ **Boxer**

▼ **Cocker
spaniel**

▲ *Hungarian puli*

▲ **Dachshund**

Getting ready

Make sure that your home is safe for the puppy. Puppies enjoy chewing electrical cords, so make sure that these are all safely tucked away.

You should also always put your toys away somewhere safe when you are done playing with them. If you leave toys lying around, your puppy might think they are toys for it to play with. Your puppy could swallow a toy and choke.

Your puppy's tail will wag a lot, and might knock things over. Make sure that any fragile objects are kept out of reach!

▲ **Make sure that there are no wires to bite and chew.**

▲ **Your puppy will run around and bump into things, so make sure that plants and decorations are not too close to the edges of tables.**

Parent Points

Never leave a puppy alone in a room. Puppies will instinctively chew anything they can get hold of—make sure that shoes, bags, and any other chewable objects are kept out of reach.

Check that there aren't any poisonous plants in the house or yard—ask your local veterinarian or nursery for advice if you're not sure.

Puppy shopping list

Your puppy will need:

◀ Two bowls: one for food and one for water—these should stand on newspaper or on a mat on the floor

▶ A special spoon or fork—always use this to serve your puppy its food

▼ A brush

▲ A dog bed—or put a soft blanket or an old bath towel in a box

◀ A pet carrier for trips to the vet and for other trips until your puppy has had its **vaccinations**

◀ **Toys for your puppy to play with**

▲ **Rubber bones and other chewy toys to keep your puppy's teeth strong and healthy**

Buy some toys and some treats for your puppy

▲ **Puppy treats**

▼ **A collar with your puppy's name and your address or phone number on it, and a leash**

Saying hello

When your puppy arrives, take it out into the yard to go to the bathroom. Do not chase it or grab it. Stay with your puppy and talk to it, so that it gets used to your voice.

Sit next to your puppy and pet it along its side, from its shoulders toward the tail. Do not pat your puppy's head.

▶ **Show your puppy where its bed is.**

▲ **Your puppy will need something to eat.**

Show your puppy where its food bowls are, and give it something to eat. Your puppy should always have fresh, clean water to drink.

Parent Points

Puppies need correct training, handling, and gentle guidance as soon as they arrive in a new home. This is to avoid bad habits and behavioral problems in the future. Training is an adult's responsibility, but the family should work as a team.

Never leave a child alone with a puppy or dog.

Handle with care

Never hit your puppy, pull its ears or tail, or throw things at it. If your puppy gets scared, it might **growl** and show its teeth. Don't go near it if it does this. Instead, back away quietly and let it calm down.

▲ **Pet your puppy very gently.**

Only pick up your puppy if you are sitting down or kneeling, otherwise, you could drop it. To pick it up, put one arm around its chest and the other hand under its rear end. Don't let its legs dangle down, and never pick it up by putting your arm around its middle.

◄ **Don't squeeze your puppy.**

▲ **Puppies need lots of sleep.**

If your puppy is asleep, don't wake it up. Don't scare it by making loud noises close by.

Parent Points
Make sure your child doesn't tease the puppy, especially by offering it food and then taking it away. This might cause the puppy to jump up and bite at the food— and at the child. Never feed your pet from the table, and never feed it chocolate. Chocolate is poisonous to dogs.

Taking care of your puppy

Once it is trained (see page 26), take your puppy for a walk at least twice a day. If your puppy gets very wet, dry it with an old towel when you get home. If it has been walking in mud, rub your puppy with an old cloth, and brush off any dried mud. Wipe your puppy's paws gently with a towel or rag.

▲ **Give your puppy special dog chews to keep its teeth strong.**

▶ **Be gentle when you brush your puppy. Do not hold it tightly or pinch it.**

Brush your puppy at least once a week. Always start at the shoulders and brush down towards the tail. Be gentle. Do not touch its head. If your puppy starts to **growl**, stop, and move away into another room.

Parent Points

Never give a puppy small or cooked bones, especially chicken bones. These can make it choke. Try giving it chew toys that look like bones instead.

The puppy should not leave the house until it has had all its vaccinations.

Never, ever leave a puppy or dog in a car on a warm or hot day, even if the windows are open. Dogs overheat very quickly.

Your puppy's life cycle

▼ A female dog can have puppies when she is between six months and one year old.

5

▶ At 10 to 18 months old, a puppy is fully grown.

4

At two weeks old, a puppy cannot see yet.

▶ **At three to four weeks old, a puppy will start being weaned from its mother's milk.**

◀ **At eight weeks old, a puppy should visit the vet for its first vaccination.**

Let's play!

Play tug of war with your puppy, using an old piece of soft cloth or a special puppy toy.

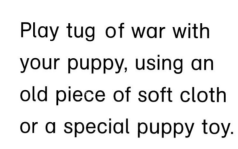

▼ **Give your puppy its own special toy.**

A puppy might bite playfully if it gets too excited. Don't hit it or yell at it—just stop playing, and leave the room.

Make sure that your puppy has some toys to play with when it is alone, so that it doesn't get bored.

▲ **Play ball with your puppy. Make sure the ball is not too big, too small, or too heavy.**

Parent Points
Always supervise your child and the puppy when they are playing together. When they play indoors, make sure that all tables and chairs are moved out of the way to avoid accidents. The puppy should be trained never to bite, even when playing, since this could lead to more aggressive behavior as the dog gets older.

Training your puppy

Teach your puppy its name. Sit or kneel in front of your puppy. Quietly say its name over and over again. When it comes to you, praise it and pet it.

Do not let your puppy jump up on the furniture when you are playing. Never hit your puppy or yell at it, even when it is naughty. When your puppy is good, give it lots of praise.

Try not to let your puppy jump up on you. Sit or kneel down to pet your puppy. Do not put your face too close to it.

Your puppy should always wear a collar with a name disc, or your vet can give it an **identity chip**.

When you take your puppy for a walk, hold on tightly to its leash. Always go out with an adult. Make sure your puppy's leash and collar are not too tight.

▲ **Your puppy will love going for walks.**

Parent Points

Make sure the puppy will heel and sits on command before letting a child walk it. An adult should always accompany the child when he or she walks the puppy.

It is advisable that all puppies and dogs wear a collar with a name disc whenever they are outside. Your vet can give the puppy an identity chip, which is a more permanent way of identifying it than a name disc.

27

Puppy watching

▲ Puppies pant when they are hot and thirsty. It helps them cool down.

◄ When a puppy comes towards you with its tail in the air, it is happy to see you.

▶ **When a puppy crouches down and wags its tail, it wants to play.**

▼ **If a puppy shows you its teeth or growls, keep away and do not touch it.**

Saying goodbye

Your puppy will grow up into an adult dog and eventually it will get old.

Many older dogs have stiff joints, and they might become ill. If this happens to your pet, keep it warm and make sure that it gets plenty of sleep. Give it lots of love, pet it gently, and talk to it quietly.

Sandy last summer

◀ **As it gets older, your dog will need shorter walks, and it will sleep more.**

My dog Sandy

Keep a special scrapbook about your pet

If your pet is very old or ill, it might die. Try not to be too sad, and remember all the fun you had together.

You might want to bury your pet in the backyard. Plant a special tree or shrub, or maybe some flowers where it is buried.

puppy checklist

Read this list and think about all the points.

✔ Puppies can't look after themselves.

✔ Cute puppies grow into dogs and can live for up to 18 years.

✔ Treat your puppy gently— as you would like to be treated yourself.

✔ Puppies have feelings, just like you.

✔ Your pet will love you very much for as long as it lives.

✔ How will you treat your puppy if it makes you mad?

✔ Don't carry your puppy around, except in an emergency.

✔ Why do you think a puppy might bite?

Parents' checklist

● **You**, not your child, are responsible for the care of the puppy.

● Dogs can be very expensive to keep. Consider the following before you commit yourself to buying a puppy:
– dog license
– veterinarian bills (seek advice from your local vet)
– food bills
– kennel or dogsitting bills when you are away
– possible training fees (some puppies may need to attend obedience classes)

● If you are out of the house for more than 3–4 hours a day, a dog is not a suitable pet.

● Do not keep even a small dog in cramped conditions.

● Are you willing to walk a dog twice a day? Your local area might also have "pooper scooper" laws.

● Do you have any other pets? Will they get along with a dog?

● Always supervise pets and children.

● If you want to buy a purebred dog, do some research first.

● All dogs need vaccinations, and worming and flea treatments. Spaying or neutering is recommended for **all** dogs. Ask your vet or local Humane Society for advice.

Puppy words

A puppy or dog can **bark** and **growl**.

A puppy's **nails** can be very sharp.

A puppy's fur is called a **coat**.

A puppy's feet are called **paws**.

A **breed** is a type of dog, such as an Alsatian or a poodle.

A **purebred** is a puppy or dog whose parents are both the same type.

A **vaccination** is a shot of medicine to prevent a puppy from getting sick.

A puppy is **weaned** when it gradually stops feeding on its mother's milk and is introduced to other foods.

Your vet can insert an **identity chip** under your puppy's skin with your pet's details on it. Vets and animal centers can "read" the chip with scanners so that lost animals can be returned home.

Kittens

Your first kitten

It's fun to have a kitten as a pet. Kittens are furry, **purry**, and playful, and wonderful to pet and cuddle.

Most cats like to play, but a fully grown cat may not be as cute and playful as a kitten.

◀ **Kittens are not toys. They can be easily hurt, and they should be treated very gently.**

▼ **A kitten needs a lot of looking after and will take up a lot of your time.**

Kittens look cute, but they grow up.

If you get bored or fed up with your pet, you can't throw it away like a toy. Cats can live for twenty years or more, so your cat may be with you for a very long time.

Which kitten?

Kittens come in all shapes, sizes and colors! They might have long or short hair and their **coat** might be plain, stripy, or patterned.

Short-haired kittens like these are easier to care for because they don't need much grooming.

Long-haired kittens need a lot of grooming.

Parent Points

Choose your kitten carefully. A long-haired kitten will be more difficult to look after as it will need regular grooming.

Some breeds of cat are more relaxed with children than others, and if you are buying a purebred cat, you should discuss this with the breeder.

If you are planning to get a rescue cat or a "mixed breed," check with the animal shelter that the cat will get on with young children. Don't buy a kitten from a pet store unless it has been recommended by your vet.

Before you buy, check that the kitten has bright, clear eyes and that it doesn't have a dirty bottom, a runny nose, or dry, dull fur.

A tabby kitten

Purebred kittens, like this Chocolate Point Siamese, are usually only available from a specialist breeder.

Lots of cats

All these cats are purebreds. A purebred cat has been bred over a long time to have certain features and colors.

▲ Maine Coon

▲ Manx

◀ Siamese

▲ Persian

▲ **Ragdoll**

◀ **Scottish Fold**

▲ **Rex**

▲ **Exotic Shorthair**

41

Kitten shopping list

Your kitten will need:

▶ A cat bed, or a box with a blanket or a towel, to sleep in

▶ A special spoon or fork—always use this to serve the cat's food

▼ Two bowls, one for water and one for food, or a double bowl

◀ **A cat carrier for trips to the vet or the cattery**

▼ **A brush**

▲ **A litter tray and some litter**

▲ **Cat toys—make sure they are not too big or too heavy for a kitten, or so small that your kitten could swallow them**

Your kitten might like some toys.

▲ **A collar for when your kitten is ready to start going outside**

Parent Points

Even if you have a backyard, you will need a litter tray for the first 14 weeks. Keep your kitten indoors until it has been fully vaccinated. The first set of vaccinations are normally done when kittens are about 12 weeks old and the second one two weeks later. You may also need to consider installing a cat flap.

Getting ready

Your kitten will race around and climb up the furniture, so make sure that there are no ornaments or plants that might fall over and get broken or hurt the kitten.

Check that your home is safe for your new kitten. Have a look around… are there any electrical cords that your kitten could chew or get tangled up in?

Before you let your kitten explore outside, be sure that it knows its name and will come when you call.

Your kitten can wear a collar with a name disc, or your vet can give it an **identity chip**.

▲ **If you give your kitten a collar, choose one with an elastic strip and put it on loosely. If the collar gets caught on anything, the kitten must be able to wriggle out of it.**

Parent Points

Check your home carefully. All sharp objects should be put away, and all houseplants should be kept out of the kitten's reach. Make sure that there are no poisonous plants in the house or yard.

Always check the washing machine and tumble drier before you turn them on, in case your kitten has crawled inside and gone to sleep.

Your vet can give the kitten an identity chip, which is a more permanent way of identifying it than a name tag.

Saying hello

Getting your first kitten is very exciting, but you must be gentle with it. When your kitten arrives in its new home, put it in a room with its bed, food, and litter tray. Leave your kitten in the room to have a good look around quietly by itself. It will explore its new surroundings and get used to all the new smells and noises.

Don't chase your kitten or grab it.
Make sure there is a box for it to
to play in, or to hide in if
it gets frightened.

Make a bed for your kitten by
putting a soft blanket or towel in a
box, or show it where its basket is.
Then show your kitten its
food bowl, and give
it a little food.

▲ **Your kitten's
bed and its food
bowl should be
somewhere quiet.**

Parent Points

Gently place the
kitten on its litter tray
as soon as it arrives, but
don't force it to sit.

A kitten may spend the first
few days hiding under a
table or behind a couch.

Make sure its food is
nearby, but leave it alone
to eat when it's ready.

Handle with care

When you pet your kitten, always start from the head and move your hand towards its tail.

Never pat your kitten hard, and never pull its tail or **whiskers**. Do not push or pull your kitten and never squeeze it.

▼ Tickle your kitten under its chin and scratch its head, but always be gentle.

◀ Some kittens like to be cradled but many don't. If your kitten starts to struggle when you pick it up or while you are holding it, put it down straight away.

When you pick up your kitten, put one hand around its front half and the other hand under its bottom. Don't let its back legs hang down. Never drop your kitten, because it may get hurt.

Parent Points

If your child is very young, make sure that he or she is sitting on a chair or on the floor when holding the kitten, as a sudden movement may make the child drop the kitten.

Make sure the child never holds the kitten too close to his or her face, as it may accidentally scratch the child. Make your child aware that kittens have very sharp claws and teeth.

Caring for your kitten

Cats and kittens like to eat regular meals. Feed your pet in the same spot and at the same time every day. A kitten needs four to five small meals every day and fresh water to drink. An adult cat can be fed once in the morning and once in the evening.

▲ **Always make sure that your kitten's food bowl is clean.**

Your kitten will need a cosy bed. Make sure that the bed is not in a draft or near a door, or in a place where people move around a lot.

◀ **Put a towel or a piece of soft blanket in a box, and place it in a quiet corner.**

Always use a special cat brush for your kitten. Brush from the head towards the tail, and don't press too hard.

If you have a long-haired kitten, you should brush it every day. A short-haired kitten should be brushed about once a week. Always use a special cat brush. If your pet has tangled fur, ask an adult to help you brush out any knots and tangles.

Your kitten's life cycle

⑤

④

▶ At five to six months old your kitten will need two to three meals a day.

1

◀ **A newborn kitten can't see, hear, or stand up.**

2

◀ **A female cat can have kittens when it is about six months old. Newborn kittens drink their mother's milk. This is called suckling.**

▲ **At three weeks old, a kitten can walk and run about and have some solid food.**

3

◀ **At ten to twelve weeks, a kitten is old enough to leave its mother.**

Let's play!

Make a toy for your kitten. If you have an old sock, put a ping-pong ball inside the toe and tie a knot in the sock. Roll this along the floor, and watch what your kitten does.

Always be gentle when you play with your kitten. Never chase it around the house or throw things at it.

Your kitten will enjoy playing with a long piece of string or yarn. You could tie a piece of string or yarn around a paper ball and pull it across the floor.

▲ **Crumple a sheet of paper into a ball, and roll it across the carpet for your kitten to chase.**

Parent Points
Never give your kitten anything to play with that is small enough to swallow. Most store-bought pet toys are safety tested but always select toys that are designed for your pet's size and age. Watch your kitten when it plays with toys.

Understanding your kitten

When your kitten **purrs**, it usually means that it is happy. But sometimes cats purr when they are nervous or in pain.

When your kitten pushes its **paws** up and down in your lap (kneading), it wants to settle down and go to sleep.

Do not make any sudden movements near your kitten. This will scare it, and it might scratch you.

Kittens have very good hearing, so never shout at your pet, make loud noises near it, or put it in a room where very loud music is being played.

Talk quietly to your kitten, and it will soon learn to recognize your voice. If you are gentle, your kitten will soon trust you.

Kitten watching

◀ When a kitten has its ears back, it is ready to attack. Keep away.

▲ When a kitten rolls on its back like this, it feels happy and safe.

▶ When a kitten rubs against you, it is leaving its scent and being friendly.

▼ When a kitten puts its bottom in the air like this, it probably wants to play.

◀ When a kitten comes towards you with its tail in the air, it is pleased to see you.

Saying goodbye

Over time, your cat will grow old and it might behave differently. As your cat gets older, it will sleep more often, move more slowly, and play less, but it will still enjoy being petted.

Many older cats have sore joints. If this happens to your pet, make sure its food, bed, and litter tray are easy to reach.

Fluffy last summer

◀ **If your cat becomes sick, make sure that it is kept warm in a quiet place.**

My cat Fluffy

Keep a special scrapbook about your pet.

If your pet is very old or ill, it may die. You will feel very sad but try to think about the happy life it shared with you.

You may say goodbye at the vet's surgery but many people bring their pet home and bury it in a special place in the yard.

Kitten checklist

Read this list, and think about all the points.

✔ Kittens have feelings, just as you do.

✔ Kittens and cats have sharp **claws** and teeth, and may scratch and bite if they are teased or they are scared. If your pet scratches you, don't hit it. Try to think about why it behaved the way it did.

✔ Cats can live for twenty years or more—will you get bored with your pet?

✔ If you care for your kitten well, it will be a friend for life.

✔ Treat your kitten gently—as you would like to be treated yourself.

✔ Never hit your pet, shout at it, drop it, chase it, or throw things at it.

✔ Kittens grow—they don't stay small and cute for ever.

Parent's checklist

● **You**, not your child, are responsible for the day-to-day care of the kitten.

● Cats are expensive pets. Work out how much it will cost to feed the kitten and pay the vet's bills. Your vet will give you advice on essential procedures, such as annual vaccinations, de-worming, and treatment for fleas.

● You shouldn't leave a cat alone for more than one night. If you go on vacation, who will look after your cat? Is there a willing neighbor who will check on and feed your cat twice a day, every day, or will the cat have to stay in a cattery? Consider the cost of a stay in a cattery—on top of the vacation.

● Some cats are more suitable for children than others. Your vet, a breeder, or the staff at an animal shelter will advise you.

● Homes with easy access to the yard are ideal for cats—but will you be happy for your kitten to use a flowerbed as a toilet? If it uses a litter tray, make sure your child does not go near it (cat feces can carry disease), and change the litter every day. Litter trays and regular supplies of litter are an additional cost.

● Never leave a very young child and a kitten alone together—they should always be supervised.

● If the kitten scratches your child, wash the scratch immediately and put antiseptic cream on it. If your child is bitten, phone your local doctor for advice—cat bites can transmit infection.

● Wherever you live, it's sensible to have your kitten neutered—whether it's male or female. Female cats can become pregnant up to three times a year and have five or six kittens in each litter.

Kitten words

Some kittens have **eyebrows**.

The long hairs on a kitten's face are called **whiskers**.

A kitten can **purr**– it makes this sound in its throat.

The sound a kitten makes is called a **meow**.

Its fur is called a **coat**.

A kitten's feet are called **paws**.

Kittens have sharp **claws**.

If you ask your vet for an **identity chip**, your contact details will be put on a microchip which the vet inserts under your pet's skin. Vets and animal shelters have scanners that 'read' the chip so that lost animals can be returned home.

A **vaccination** is an injection to stop your kitten from catching serious diseases.

Hamsters
and Gerbils

Your first hamster or gerbil

Hamsters and gerbils are lively little animals, and they love to play. Hamsters are nocturnal. This means that they like to sleep during the day and wake up at night.

▼ **Hamsters and gerbils are small and fragile.**

Hamsters and gerbils are very small and can easily get hurt. You should always handle them gently.

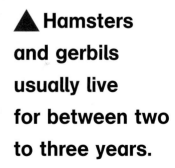

▲ **Hamsters and gerbils usually live for between two to three years.**

Which pet?

Gerbils are very active and do not like to be alone. It is best to buy two brothers or two sisters and keep them together.

▲ Hamsters like to live alone.

Hamsters sleep during the day and wake up at night, so you will not be able to play with your hamster in the daytime.

▼ Do not mix gerbils and hamsters together.

Lots of pets

There are many different **breeds** of hamster and gerbil. They have different colored fur and different markings.

◀ **Black Mongolian gerbil**

▶ **Agouti Syrian hamster**

▼ **Lilac Mongolian gerbil**

◀ Black Syrian hamster

▶ Albino gerbils

▲ Golden Satin Syrian hamster

Your shopping list

Your hamster or gerbils will need:

◀ Shredded white paper towels and a small cardboard box. Never use newspaper

▼ Or you could use hay...

...or wood shavings. Never use cedar or pine.

▼ A cage or a plastic tank

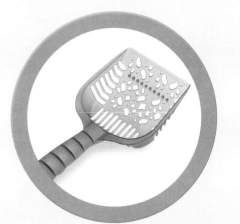

► **Hamster food or gerbil food**

▲ **A scoop for cleaning out the tank**

◄ **A food bowl and a water bottle with a metal spout**

Your pet will enjoy some toys

Getting ready

The best home for a hamster or some gerbils is a plastic tank or a wire cage with a solid floor. It should be big enough for your pet to run around in.

Cover the floor with a layer of wood shavings. Add little piles of hay or shredded white paper towel so that your pet can make a cozy nest.

▲ **Gerbils will often make a cozy nest from the material you put in their tank.**

▲ **Make sure your hamster's tank or cage has a separate cozy nest box.**

74

Saying hello

When your pet first comes to live at your house, it might feel very scared. Place it gently in its tank or cage, and leave it alone for a couple of hours to get used to its new home.

Do not make any loud noises near it. Talk to it quietly, so that it gets to know your voice.

Do not make any loud noises or sudden movements near your pet.

Soon, your pet will start to explore its new home and will enjoy running up and down ladders in its cage or tank.

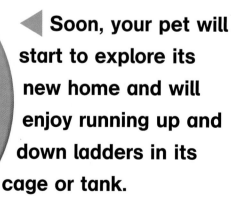

Offer your pet a treat, such as a piece of apple. After a couple of days, your pet will start to get used to you and will let you cup it in your hand.

Parent Points
Make sure your child knows how to handle the hamster or gerbil before he or she tries to pick it up (see pages 78-79).

Handle with care

Hamsters and gerbils are very small, and a hand swooping down from above will scare them. Slowly put your closed hand into the tank or cage, and let your pet sniff it. Gently open your hand, and let your pet climb onto your palm.

▲ **Always use two hands to hold your pet.**

◀ **To pick up your pet, gently scoop it into your palm. Never grab your pet around its body or dangle it by its tail.**

Always sit or kneel down when you are holding or playing with your pet so that you don't drop it. Hold your pet gently. Never squeeze it.

Feeding your pet

◀ **Your pet should always have some food. Buy special hamster or gerbil food from a pet store or vet.**

▲ **Carrot-shaped wood chew block**

Feed your pet a piece of fresh fruit or vegetable every day. Try carrot, apple, celery, broccoli, banana, or cucumber.

As a treat, hide a piece of a plain cracker or dry bread in the cage for your pet to find. Never give it candy or sticky food.

Broccoli

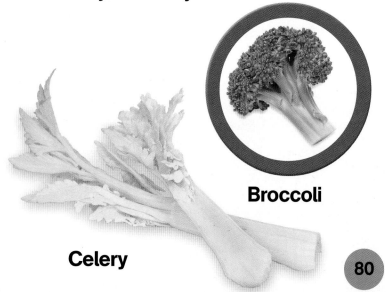

Celery

Make sure your pet has a block of wood to gnaw on. This will help to keep its teeth short and healthy.

Make sure your pet's water bottle always has plenty of clean water in it.

Apple

Carrot

Parent Points

Do not feed hamsters and gerbils too much green food, because this can cause diarrhea. Never change your pet's diet suddenly; if you need to make a change, do so gradually over a few days. Do not feed either hamsters or gerbils acidic fruits such as oranges or strawberries.

Keep it clean

Your hamster's and gerbils' tank or cage needs to be kept clean. Once a day, use the scoop to clear out droppings and old bits of food.

Give the tank or cage a really good clean with a little animal-safe disinfectant once a week. Wipe all the surfaces, and wash the toys.

Give your hamster's home a really good clean every week. You should clean out your gerbil's home every two weeks.

Wash the food bowl every day. Clean out the water bottle with a bottle brush once a week.

Always wash your hands when you are done cleaning out the tank.

Parent Points
Use animal-safe disinfectant (available from pet stores) for cleaning the tank. Make sure the pet is put somewhere safe while its home is being cleaned.

Your gerbil's life cycle

⑤

▶ When a female gerbil is about three months old, she can have babies. Her babies drink her milk. This is called suckling.

◀ At six weeks old, a gerbil is old enough to leave its mother.

④

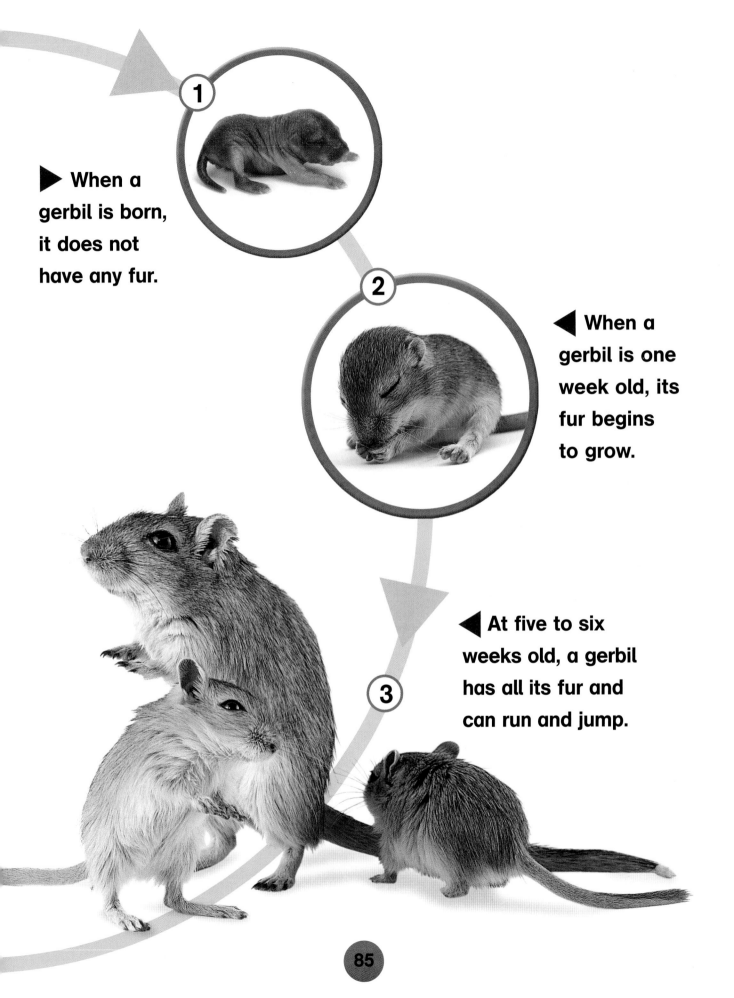

▶ When a gerbil is born, it does not have any fur.

1

2

◀ When a gerbil is one week old, its fur begins to grow.

◀ At five to six weeks old, a gerbil has all its fur and can run and jump.

3

Let's play!

Gerbils and hamsters are very active, so give your pet some toys. Put some cardboard tubes in the tank or cage. Cut holes in a plastic bottle for your pet to explore.

Hide food for your pet to find.

▼ **Your pet will love to climb in and out of holes.**

▶ As a treat, buy your pet a special habitat. You'll enjoy watching it have fun.

▲ Only give your pet hamster a solid wheel because your pet's tail or legs could get trapped in an open wheel. Do not give a wheel to your pet gerbil.

Parent Points
Hamsters and gerbils should be allowed out of the tank or cage once a day, so that they can get some exercise. Make a playground in a large cardboard box with some toys. Make sure your pet cannot escape into corners, under doors, behind baseboards, up fire places, or into pieces of furniture. Keep cats and dogs out of the room.

Make a

Make a playground for your pet to exercise in. Use an old cardboard box, old toilet paper tubes, old paper towel tubes, and some cartons.

playground

Saying goodbye

Pets get older, just as people do. As your pet grows older, it will play less and spend more time sleeping. Don't give it as much food as before, or it will get fat.

My pet Cuddles

◀ **If your pet is ill, or appears to be in pain, take it to the veterinarian.**

90

Gerbils and hamsters have shorter life-spans than some other family pets. So your child is likely to be quite young when he or she has to confront death for the first time.

If one gerbil from a pair dies, give the surviving pet lots of attention. Do not replace its companion straight away.

Cuddles last summer

Keep a special scrapbook about your pet

Gerbils and hamsters live for two or three years, so one day the time will come to say goodbye.

It is sad when a pet dies. Making a scrapbook all about your pet might help you feel better.

Pet checklist

Read this list, and think about all the points.

✔ Treat your pet gently —as you would like to be treated yourself.

✔ Hamsters and gerbils are not toys.

✔ Gerbils and hamsters are very small and can easily get hurt if you are not gentle.

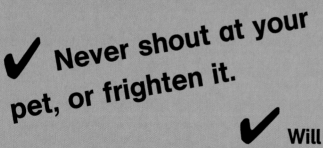

✔ How will you treat your pet if it makes you angry?

✔ Never shout at your pet, or frighten it.

✔ Animals can feel pain, just as you do.

✔ Will you be happy to clean out your pet's cage or tank every day?

Parents' checklist

- **You**, not your child, are responsible for the care of the pet.

- Your pet will need someone to look after it every day when you are away from home—this includes feeding, cleaning, and exercising.

- Hamsters and gerbils are small pets, and can easily get stepped on—make sure your child is aware of the dangers.

- Exercise wheels are not appropriate toys for gerbils as their tails can become trapped.

- Hamsters will bite if they are scared or angry.

- Hamsters should be left to sleep during the day. Don't keep two hamsters together, even if they are from the same litter.

- Never use newspaper in your pet's cage—it is poisonous to both hamsters and gerbils.

- Always supervise pets and children.

- If hamsters get too cold, they may go into hibernation and appear dead. Cup your hamster gently in your hands to warm it up.

Pet words

The fur of a hamster or gerbil is called its **coat**.

A gerbil has a long **tail**.

A hamster has hardly any **tail**.

The long hairs on the face of a hamster or gerbil are called **whiskers**.

Hamsters and gerbils have **claws** on their toes.

A **breed** is a special type of hamster or gerbil, such as a Black Mongolian gerbil or Black Syrian hamster.

Index